MUSIC READINESS SERIES

MY FIRST MUSIC BOOK

by
Betty Glasscock and Jay Ste
in collaboration with David Car
editorial assistance by Carole F
illustrations by Bob Blansky

FOREWORD

MY FIRST MUSIC BOOK introduces the very young child to the world of music, a world to be shared by the child, parent and teacher. The book is designed to utilize the energy, enthusiasm and creativeness of children in developing musical awareness and participation as they listen to the sounds of music, respond to its rhythms and learn its written symbols.

Motor skill development is carefully structured throughout the series, with activities geared to the young child's physical capabilities. Concepts are introduced gradually, well before the child is expected to recognize the symbols or relate them to the keyboard.

TO THE PARENT: Your role is very important. You will need to spend some musical awareness time with your child every day to reinforce the concepts presented during the lesson. The teacher will give you specific instructions so that you will know each week what is expected of you. You will also find a section directed to you in each of the nine program guides beginning on page 30.

You will notice that all the directions on the activity pages are directed to the child. Although unable to read them, even the young child will follow along as you and the teacher explain them, thus increasing general reading readiness skills.

TO THE TEACHER: This book is designed in nine programs, each dealing with specific integrated concepts. Do not consider one program to necessarily be one lesson. Adjust the program division to meet the specific needs of your class. General suggestions are on page 29; lesson activities and planning helps for each of the programs begin on page 30.

TO THE TEACHER AND PARENT: The CASSETTE TAPE RECORDING of the MUSIC READINESS SERIES includes all the keyboard and singing songs. The songs are presented in sequential order as their titles or page references appear in the Program Guide, pages 30-47.

This recording will be helpful to the teacher in class as melodic lines, rhythm ensembles, or suggested body movements are demonstrated and explored with the songs.

Listening to the recording at home will aid the parent and student as words, rhythms, and melodies of the songs are reinforced.

> The code at the bottom of the student page will direct you to the related material in the teacher's section. For example (PI-30A) indicates "Refer to Program I, page 30, Activity A."

The MUSIC READINESS SERIES continues with
MY COLOR AND PLAY BOOK - A   and MY PIANO BOOK - A
MY COLOR AND PLAY BOOK - B   and MY PIANO BOOK - B

Special thanks to teachers and students of the Glover Music Village for their willingness and enthusiasm in testing this series.

CONTENTS

Bobby and Bonnie Bear are watching the Three Little Monkeys play on the MAGICAL, MARVELOUS, MAGNIFICENT, MUSICAL RAINBOW. Bobby and Bonnie and the Three Little Monkeys are going to show you many things about music. We are going to play on the rainbow with them. Color this beautiful picture.

4

Some things make HIGH sounds. Some things make LOW sounds. Which of these things make high sounds? Which of them make low sounds?

1. Color each picture.

2. Cut out each block and place it on your keyboard in the place for high or low sounds.

See FOREWORD page 1 for explanation of this cue: (PI-30E)

High, Middle, Low

High in the treetop
Baby birds sing!

And from a big limb...
Boys and girls swing!

Cows eating green grass
make a low moo!

I can make high and Low sounds too!

LEFT HAND

1. Place your LEFT HAND over the bass clef sign.
2. Draw around your hand. Your teacher will help you.

(PII-32E)

RIGHT HAND

---

1. Place your RIGHT HAND over the treble clef sign.
2. Draw around your hand. Your teacher will help you.

(PII-32E)

TWO BLACK KEYS

1. Color Bobby and Bonnie.
2. Locate and play all the groups of TWO BLACK KEYS on the keyboard.

the two black keys are
BoBBY and BoNNiE

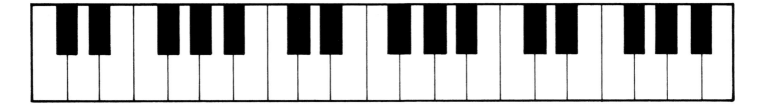

1. Circle all the groups of TWO BLACK KEYS.
2. Color Bobby and Bonnie Bear.

(PIII-34C)

Color this QUARTER NOTE black.

MARCHING BEARS

1
CLAP

1
CLAP

1
CLAP

1
CLAP

1. Color the bears.
2. Color the quarter notes BLACK.
3. Clap and count the quarter notes aloud. Say "One one one one."

(PIV-36A)

BOBBY'S MAGICAL

Bobby is working some magic for us,
Watch what he can do.
With lines and spaces, a bar and a brace,
He's making a grand staff for you!
A treble clef sign and a bass clef sign
Will show us high and low.
With a flick of his musical, magical wand
A GRAND STAFF appears - - HO! HO!

Draw a line from these parts of the grand staff to those on the next page.

(PV-38A)

Up, up, up, up,
Oh, so high!
Climbing, climbing
In the sky.
Up, up, up, up,
Never stop!
Higher, higher,
POP!

1. With your YELLOW crayon, color the word "UP" and the arrow pointing UP.
2. Draw a YELLOW circle around the group of notes that move UP.
3. With your GREEN crayon, color the word "DOWN" and the arrow pointing DOWN.
4. Draw a GREEN circle around the group of notes that move DOWN.

1. Here are some things that go up and down. Color the pictures.
2. Make up a story about these things. Your teacher will help you.

Cut out the picture blocks.

(PVI-40D)

EL 3143

TREBLE CLEF
IT TELLS US TO PLAY HIGH SOUNDS

BASS CLEF
IT TELLS US TO PLAY LOW SOUNDS

QUARTER NOTE
IT RECEIVES ONE (1) BEAT

LEFT HAND

RIGHT HAND

GRAND STAFF

BIG BASS DRUM
IT MAKES LOW SOUNDS

FLUTE
IT MAKES HIGH SOUNDS

QUARTER NOTES GOING UP

TWO BLACK KEYS
BOBBY AND BONNIE LIVE HERE

1. With your RED crayon, color the word "LOUD."
2. With your BLUE crayon, color the word "SOFT."
3. Draw a RED circle around each of the things that make LOUD sounds.
4. Draw a BLUE circle around each of the things that make SOFT sounds.

(PVII-42B)

THREE BLACK KEYS

1. Color the Three Little Monkeys
2. Locate and play all the groups of THREE BLACK KEYS on the keyboard.

(PVII-42C)

The three black keys are the
THREE LiTTLE MONKEYS...

1. Circle all the groups of THREE BLACK KEYS.
2. Color the Three Little Monkeys.

(PVII-42C)

BLACK KEY GROUPS

1. On the top keyboard, circle all the groups of TWO BLACK KEYS.
2. On the bottom keyboard, circle all the groups of THREE BLACK KEYS.

(PVII-42E)

With your black crayon draw on the dotted lines to make the head of this half note. Color the stem black. Be sure to leave the middle of the note WHITE.

(PVII-42H)

RHYTHM PATTERNS

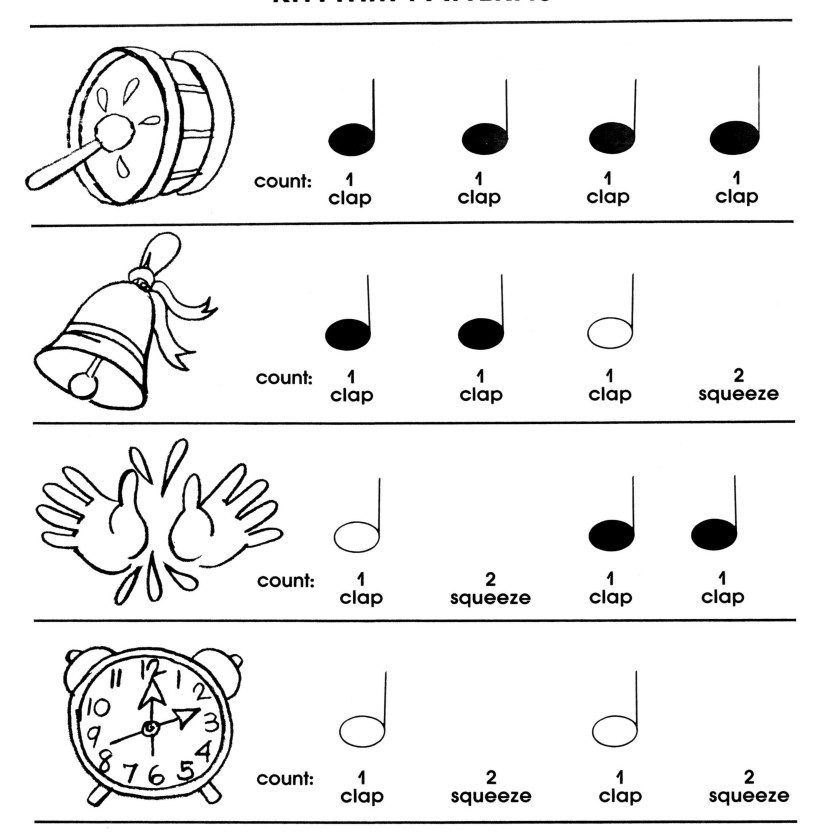

count: 1   1   1   1
        clap   clap   clap   clap

count: 1   1   1   2
        clap   clap   clap   squeeze

count: 1   2   1   1
        clap   squeeze clap   clap

count: 1   2   1   2
        clap   squeeze clap   squeeze

1. Clap and count aloud these rhythm patterns. Keep a steady pulse.
2. Play the patterns on rhythm instruments.
3. Repeat each pattern many times.

(PVIII-44A)

LINE and SPACE NUMBERS

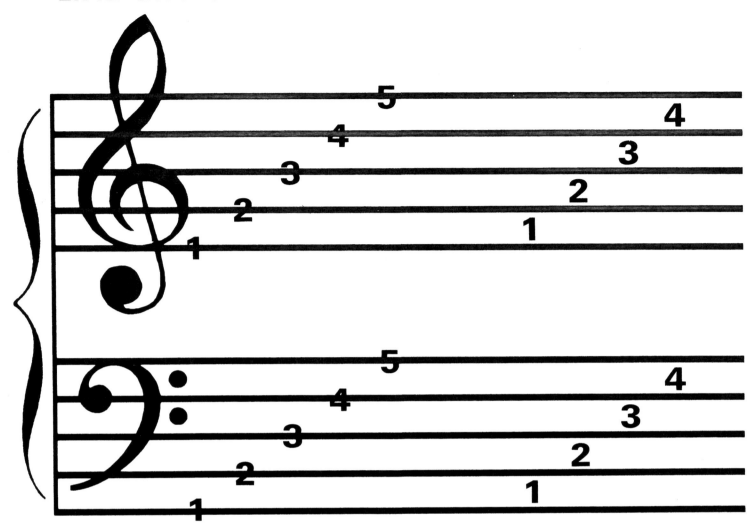

LINE and SPACE NOTES

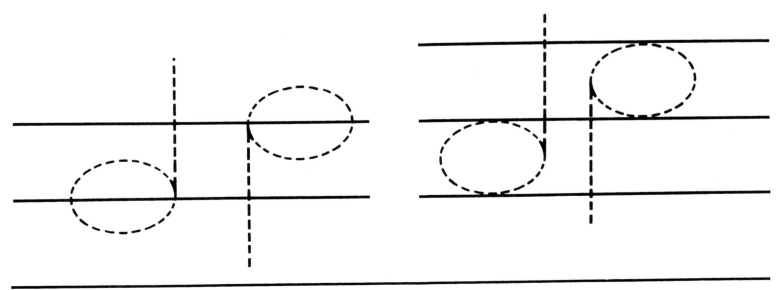

1. Point to each LINE on the grand staff and say its number.
2. Point to each SPACE on the grand staff and say its number.
3. Draw on the dotted lines to make LINE notes. Color one note BLACK.
4. Draw on the dotted lines to make SPACE notes. Color one note BLACK.

(PIX-46A)

NOTES ON THE GRAND STAFF

1. Color the notes BLACK and cut them out. Your teacher or parent may help you.
2. Place the notes on different lines and spaces of the grand staff.
3. Say the number of the line or space where you placed each note.
   Say whether the note is on the treble or bass staff.

(PIX-46C)

The student is now ready for MY PIANO BOOK A and MY COLOR AND PLAY BOOK A.

This certificate is presented to

In Recognition of the
Successful Completion of

MY FIRST MUSIC BOOK

By Betty Glasscock
and Jay Stewart
in collaboration with
DAVID CARR GLOVER

Teacher

Date

Guidelines for MY FIRST MUSIC BOOK

Parental involvement is essential; parents must work with the children during the week. This is done most effectively if the parent attends the weekly lesson. Parents' responsibilities for daily reinforcement of concepts are listed in each Program, beginning on page 30.

Young children have short attention spans requiring a variety of activities. Change often from physical activities to quiet ones.

Big-muscle movement works best. Have children make BIG movements to the music. Have them march, swing arms, or bend. At the keyboard, arms or fists first work better than individual fingers.

Singing is a wonder-worker for ear training, rhythmic feel, dramatics. Plan to do much singing. Be sure to schedule time for listening to recordings. A list of suggested recordings is on page 48.

Rhythm instruments need not be fancy or expensive to be fun and effective. You can make a drum from an oatmeal box, maracas from dried gourds, a triangle from a very large nail held by a string and struck with another nail, cymbals from kettle lids.

A floor keyboard or staff can be made by making lines with permanent markers or black tape on white plastic. Rhythm charts can be made on newsprint or inexpensive art paper bought by the roll. Put charts on bulletin boards, tape them to the walls, hang them from tables. Keep them visible.

Don't hesitate to improvise; children will readily accept what you provide them to play with, see and touch.

Be sure the children understand the words you use. Music is a new language to them; don't assume anything. Be prepared to continually review and reinforce.

Let the children discover the things you want them to know. Ask questions; they'll find the answers and remember them.

Be generous with praise. It is vital that the child's first structured experiences with music be pleasant, successful and fulfilling. Every criticism should be balanced with praise for something done well.

Be flexible with your planning and teaching; be ready to take advantage of the spontaneity and natural creativity of the children. Use this experience to expand your own creativeness. Make up songs for your class - you can do it! Experiment, keeping the concepts always in mind. Additional black key songs are included on page 47; create more of your own for your class if you wish to do more keyboard work at this level.

Have fun! The impressions that you create for the students will be with them forever. Make this the most exciting and enjoyable teaching you've ever done!

Specific teaching suggestions are given in the PROGRAMS which begin on page 30. The concepts emphasized in MY FIRST MUSIC BOOK of The **MUSIC READINESS SERIES** are presented in nine programs. A program may require several lessons; adapt the programs to fit the needs of your students.

PROGRAM I
Student page 4

CONCEPTS: High and low sounds
MOTOR SKILLS: Clapping and marching to a steady beat
LISTENING: Hearing high and low sounds

ACTIVITIES

A. Teach "If You're Happy", page 31 with actions.

B. Ask questions about how music makes students feel and about their favorite songs.

C. Sing some familiar songs, page 31.
Have students clap a steady pulse; relate pulse to heartbeat.
Have students feel the pulse of songs by walking, swinging arms, playing rhythm instruments while teacher plays on keyboard or uses records.

D. Have students name things that make high sounds (birds, whistles). Stretch arms high. For low sounds (cows, frogs, trucks) - stoop low.

Play keyboard sounds as children stretch or stoop, relating high-low to the keyboard.
Have students play high-low on keyboard.
    NOTE: If students mention middle sounds, have them put their hands on their knees and bend knees slightly. Play middle sounds on keyboard. (Middle sounds will be used in Program Two.)

E. Help students color and cut page 4. Coloring must ALWAYS emphasize the musical concept; continue to direct students' thoughts as they color. (Some coloring may be done at home).
Have students place the pictures on high-low areas of keyboard.
If you have a floor keybaord, have students stand, march, put pictures on high-low.

F. Teach "Let's March", page 30.   1. sing words
                                      2. sing and clap a steady pulse
                                      3. march and sing

G. Teach "Say Goodbye" page 31. This song will always be the signal for students to put away their things, make a circle and sing the song. It means the lesson is over.

DAILY HOME ASSIGNMENTS for student and parent

1. Help the student listen for high and low sounds on TV, radio, household appliances, animal sounds and other things you can hear around you.

2. Make high-low sounds at the keyboard—it makes no difference which keys or how many at a time, or with which fingers. Clusters (several keys) are fine; they may be played with fist or arm. The high or low sounds are the important things this week.

4. Sing together as much as you can. Don't be self-conscious; your child will love singing with you.

Let's March

B. GLASSCOCK

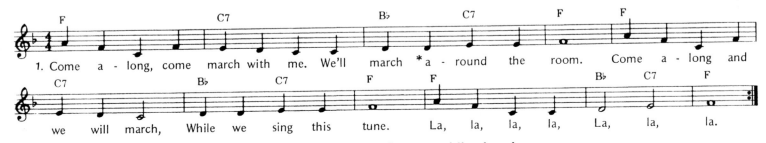

*2. around the high keys   3. around the low keys
4. around the treble clef   4. around the bass clef

Twinkle Twinkle

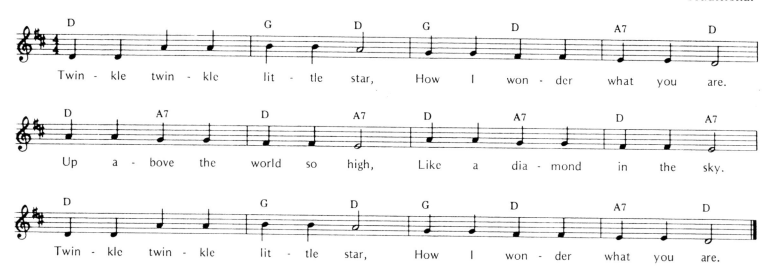

Mary Had a Little Lamb

Traditional

Say Goodbye

B. GLASSCOCK

If You're Happy

PROGRAM II
Student pages 5-7

CONCEPTS: Identifying right and left hands

MOTOR SKILLS: Responding to steady beat by marching, clapping, playing rhythm instruments

LISTENING: Reinforcement of high-low sounds
Reinforcement of hearing and feeling steady pulse

ACTIVITIES

A. Sing and play "I Put My Right Hand In", page 33.
Play Simon Says game. Students do everything that Simon says to do. If teacher gives directions without saying "Simon says..." the students are NOT to follow directions and are out of the game if they do. Play a few practice games first.

B. Teach "High-Low Poem" as directed on page 33.

C. Keyboard work: have student play steady quarter note pulse with right hand, any keys, fist or fingers. Repeat, using left hand.
As student plays a key, teacher could play a song that everyone has clapped.
Students not at the keyboard should clap and sing.

D. Use picture cards from page 4 in guiding students to make high-low keyboard sounds. Place cards and/or students on floor keyboard.
NOTE: Make a durable set of cards by backing them with cardboard and covering them with clear Contac paper.

E. Help students complete pages 6 and 7 as you relate clef signs to high-low sounds. Use floor staff and large clef signs if you have them. Have students place high-low pictures on clef signs.

F. Sing "Let's March", page 30. Have a parade, singing and using rhythm instruments. Have students take turns being leader. On second line sing "We're marching on the bass clef" or "high keys" or "treble clef."

G. Teach "The People on the Bus", page 33. Place chairs as seats on a bus. (Find out if any of the children have been on a bus.) Have students decide on appropriate actions.

Don't forget about the "Say Goodbye" song.

DAILY HOME ASSIGNMENTS for student and parent

1. Learn words to the "High Low Poem" on page 5. Say it with a steady beat.

CLAP   X   X   X   X   X   X   X   X

2. High in the tree tops baby birds sing, And from a big limb boys and girls swing. etc.
Clap the rhythm together as you both say the words. Do it slowly.

3. Student may experiment with keyboard sounds to match the poem, using any keys, trying to keep the beat steady. (Don't expect perfection; coordination is developing.)

4. Help student identify Right Hand and Left Hand.

I Put My Hand Right In

singing game

1. I put my *right hand in. I take my right hand out. I

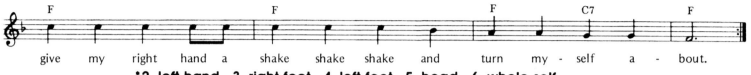

give my right hand a shake shake shake and turn my-self a-bout.

*2. left hand   3. right foot   4. left foot   5. head   6. whole self

The People On The Bus

children's play song

1. The peo-ple on the bus go up and down, up and down, up and

down. The peo-ple on the bus go up and down, all o-ver town.____

2. horn on the bus goes beep, beep, beep.   3. wipers on the bus go swish, swish, swish.
4. money in the box goes clink, clink, clink. 5. baby on the bus goes waah, waah, waah.
6. mother on the bus goes shh, shh, shh.   7. wheels on the bus go round and round.
8. driver on the bus says move on back.

High, Middle, Low

DIRECTIONS: 1. Teacher and students chant the words and clap the first beat of each measure.
2. Teacher and students chant the words and do body movements as indicated.
3. Teacher plays piano and chants the words while students chant and do the body movements.
(Each procedure could require several sessions.)

PROGRAM III
Student pages 8-9

CONCEPTS: Groups of two black keys
              Finger numbers

MOTOR SKILLS: Clapping, marching, playing rhythm instruments

LISTENING: Hearing fast and slow rhythms

ACTIVITIES

A.   Sing "Where is Thumbkin", page 35.
        Help students put finger numbers on drawings, pages 6 and 7.

B.   Teach "ALL ABOARD", page 35.
        Have the students make a train and move around the room as they sing this song. Have them move their arms like the wheels of the train. Choose a "conductor" to call out, "All aboard", before the song. The conductor may call out the name of your town as the train comes into the station. Name two places in the room "train stations". The train leaves the first station slowly, increases speed, then goes slower as it approaches the other station.

C.   Have students complete page 8 as directed.
        Students locate all groups of two black keys on floor keyboard and/or keyboard.
        Help students count the groups.
        Students complete page 9 as directed.
        With fist of right hand student plays each group of two black keys, starting with the lowest group, chanting, "Bobby Bonnie" as indicated.
        Repeat with left hand, going down the keyboard, continuing the chanting.

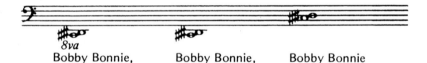

      Bobby Bonnie,   Bobby Bonnie,   Bobby Bonnie

     Students play the groups of two black keys while chanting the "High Low Poem", page 5. Use right hand on high keys, either hand on middle keys, left hand on low keys.
     (Additional Black Key Songs—47)

D.   See LISTENING SUGGESTIONS page 48.

DAILY HOME ASSIGNMENTS for student and parent

1.   Together say the words to "High Low Poem" on page 5 as student plays the groups of two black keys on high-middle-low areas of the keyboard. Student may use either fingers 2 and 3 or the fist to play the keys.

2.   Listen for slow and fast sounds such as different speeds of mixer, different kinds of music on TV, commercials, records, walking or running sounds.

3.   Review finger numbers and right and left hands.

4.   Sing!

Where Is Thumbkin?

finger game

Where is Thumb-kin, Where is Thumb-kin? Here I am. Here I am.
(fin - ger num - ber one _____)

How are you to-day sir? Ver - y well, I thank you. Run a - way Run a - way.

Where is Thumbkin?

Sing: Where is finger number one? (two, etc.)
Action: Put both hands behind back.

Sing: Here I am.
Actions: Bring right hand to the front, holding up correct finger.

Sing: Here I am.
Action: Bring left hand to the front, holding up correct finger.

Sing: How are you today, sir?
Action: Make right hand finger bow to left hand.

Sing: Very well, I thank you.
Action: Make left hand finger bow to right hand.

Sing: Run away.
Action: Put right hand behind back.

Sing: Run away.
Action: Put left hand behind back.

Continue for each of the finger numbers.

Oats, Peas, Beans and Barley Grow

action song

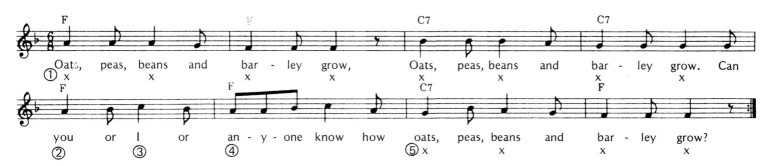

Oats, peas, beans and bar - ley grow, Oats, peas, beans and bar - ley grow. Can
① x   x   x   x   x   x   x   x

you or I or an - y - one know how oats, peas, beans and bar - ley grow?
②   ③   ④   ⑤ x   x   x   x

Oats, Peas, Beans and Barley Grow

Have students stand in a circle.
Directions for actions for verse one match number on the music.

① clap pulse (x)
② point to someone in the circle
③ point to yourself
④ hold hands palms up
⑤ clap pulse (x)

Second verse: (sing words)
① "First the farmer sows his seed,
② Then he stands and takes his ease,
③ Stamps his foot and claps his hand
④ And turns about to view his land."

Actions for the second verse:
① Pretend to hold seed bag in left arm. Reach in bag with right hand and sow seed.
② Fold arms across chest and put the right foot out, resting on the heel.
③ Stamp foot and clap hands
④ Hold right hand to shade eyes and turn around

All Aboard

D.C. GLOVER

Conductor calls out, "All Aboard"

Chug, chug, chug, chug, Puff, puff, puff, puff, Rid - ing down the track.

Toot, toot, toot, toot, Clang, clang, clang, clang. Round the bend we're com - ing back.

PROGRAM IV
Student pages 10-11

CONCEPTS: Quarter note

MOTOR SKILLS: Playing a steady quarter note beat on the groups of two black keys and on rhythm instruments

LISTENING: Music used in telling a story

ACTIVITIES

A.   Introduce the quarter note. What does it look like?
As students color the quarter note on page 10 and the marching bears on page 11, relate quarter notes to marching. Play marching music for students to listen to.
Have students march as they clap and count aloud-"one, one, one, one."
Draw quarter notes on chalkboard. Have students play rhythm instruments and count "one" for each quarter note.
Make rhythm charts from poster board, newsprint or flannel board. Clap and count.

Teach "Quarter Note March", page 37.
   1. Clap and sing
   2. March and sing
   3. March, sing, and play rhythm instruments-that makes a parade!

B.   Review finger numbers.
Teach "Here is the Beehive", page 37. Make a hive by putting fists together with fingers inside. As students sing the numbers they let the fingers out of the hive. After they know the song, try mixing up the numbers: "two, four, five, three, one."

C.   Play the FISH GAME. **Directions:** Cut fish shapes from colored paper. Draw music symbols, notes and rhythm patterns on the fish. Put a paper clip at the nose of each fish. Use a large plastic bowl or a box as a "fishbowl." Tie a string to a dowel and put a large magnet on the end of the string as a hook.
The student "fishes." When the fish is caught, the student must name the symbol or note or count and clap the rhythm pattern. If the answer is correct, the student keeps the fish for the rest of the game. If not correct, the fish must be put back into the fishbowl. The student with the most fish at the end of the game is the winner. NOTE: Additional fish should be added as students learn more symbols and rhythm patterns.

D.   See LISTENING SUGGESTIONS page 48.

DAILY HOME ASSIGNMENTS for student and parent

1.   Sing "Where is Thumbkin", page 35, and "Here is the Beehive", page 37.
2.   Have students practice drawing quarter notes. The stem goes up on the right side, down on the left side of the note.
3.   Student should play the groups of two black keys, up and down, fast and slow.

Here Is The Beehive

traditional

Here is the bee - hive, where are the bees? Hid - den a - way where no - bod - y sees.

Watch and you'll see them come out of the hive, One, two, three, four, five.

Quarter Note March

B. GLASSCOCK

Quarter note march - ing, One one one one. Quarter note march - ing, All a - round.

PROGRAM V
Student pages 12 and 13

CONCEPTS: Grand staff
Location of high and low sounds on the grand staff

MOTOR SKILLS: Finger number responses
Matching body movements to rhythms of quarters, eighths and dotted half notes

LISTENING: Hearing different rhythms and responding with body movements

ACTIVITIES

A.   Introduce the students to the grand staff.
Have students put the high-low sound pictures from program one on the floor staff in correct areas.
Use pages 12-13 to teach the parts of the grand staff.

B.   Teach "Skating Song", page 39.
Have students "skate" to the dotted half note rhythm.

C.   Play examples of different rhythms. Have students make marching movements to the quarter notes, running movements to eighth notes, and skating movements to the dotted half notes. NOTE: Students are asked only to hear the different kinds of notes; they are not asked to identify them.

D.   Sing "This Old Man", page 39. Have students decide which motions to use for each verse.
Use rhythm instruments to accompany the song, adding an instrument for each verse.

E.   Have the students move the way they think different things move: puppet, baby chick, scarecrow, elephant, big bear, grasshopper. Teacher may play appropriate rhythms as students move.

F.   See LISTENING SUGGESTIONS page 48.

DAILY HOME ASSIGNMENTS for student and parent

1.   Review names of the parts of the grand staff as shown on pages 12 and 13.

2.   Sing "Here is the Beehive" often, page 37.

3.   Review the keyboard activities from previous lessons. Student may be ready to experiment with more sounds and rhythms.

This Old Man

English Folk Song

1. This old man, He played one, He played nick nack on my thumb, with a

nick nack pad - dy wack, give the dog a bone, This old man came roll - ing home.

2. This old man, he played two, He played nick, nack on my shoe.

3. This old man, he played three, He played nick nack on my knee.

4. This old man, he played four, He played nick, nack on my door.

(Make other verses if you wish.)

Skating Song

J. Stewart

Skat - ing, glid - ing, Reach for the tre - ble clef high. _____

Swoop - ing, slid - ing, Down to the bass clef we glide. _____

PROGRAM VI
Student pages 14-18

CONCEPTS: Notes go up and down
We read notes from left to right

MOTOR SKILLS: Reinforcement of acquired skills
Evaluation of students' responding with steady rhythms in marching,
clapping, playing rhythm instruments, action games and songs

LISTENING: Deciding which sounds to use to help tell a story

ACTIVITIES

A. Teach "Notes Can Go Up" poem, page 14. KEEP IT SLOW!
   1. Teacher and students chant the words in rhythm, clapping on first beat of measure.
   2. Student plays the groups of two black keys with fist while chanting the words.
      Keys are to be played as cluster, not separately.
   3. Have students decide what to do for the "Pop" sound.
      NOTE: Each procedure could require several sessions.

Up Up Up Up   Oh so high,   Climbing climbing   In the sky.   Up Up Up Up   Nev-er stop.   High-er high-er   Pop!

B. Students complete page 15 as directed.
   Use quarter note rhythm chart or chalkboard to help establish left to right reading.
   Point to each note as students clap or play rhythm instruments. Students can take turns being the leader.

C. As students color the pictures on page 16 help them create a story about all the things in the picture. Have them decide which sounds they can use to help tell the story. Practice telling the story. Teacher may be the storyteller, using the sounds they have chosen. (Think sound effects, such as crinkling paper for leaves.)
   Record the story and play it back. (Students might like to perform the story for another class or for guests.) Have fun with the story and the sounds!

D. Use flash cards on page 17 for review. NOTE: Make a set of larger flash cards like the ones on page 17 (5 x 5 is a good size) for use in class. Draw the pictures on heavy paper, back with cardboard and laminate with clear Contac paper.

   Make a book pocket for flash cards. Cut one end from an envelope and tape the three closed sides to the inside of the book cover. Cut the front piece in a half-moon shape to make it easier to get the flash cards in and out.

E. Use the songs on page 41 to reinforce use of motions, sounds and dramatics with the rhythms of the music. Two or three students could prepare a song with motions, sounds or dramatics to perform for the rest of the class. Take turns.

DAILY HOME ASSIGNMENTS for student and parent

1. Together chant the words to "Notes Can Go Up" poem, page 14.

2. Student should play the groups of two black keys up the keyboard with left hand, then right hand, fingers or fist. Try to keep a steady beat. (Don't have the student sitting on the bench to do these.)

3. Have student make up stories about page 16. (These might be the same story over and over - that's fine.) Experiment with sounds for the story.

4. Play "Simon Says" using fingers as well as arms and legs. Take turns being Simon. **(PII-32A)**

The Eensie Weensie Spider

① The Een-sie Ween-sie spi-der went up the wa-ter spout.

② Down came the rain___ ③ and washed the spi-der out.

④ Out came the sun___ and ⑤ dried up all the rain; ⑥ Now

Een-sie Ween-sie spi-der went up the spout a-gain.

THE EENSIE WEENSIE SPIDER
① Make fingers climb up in air.
② Wiggle fingers downward to make raindrops.
③ Put hands together and bring down quickly to "wash the spider out."
④ Circle arms above head.
⑤ Wiggle fingers while lifting arms to "dry up all the rain."
⑥ Make fingers climb up in the air.

I'm a Little Teapot

I'm a lit-tle tea-pot, Short and stout, ① Here's my han-dle, ② Here's my spout.

When I get all steamed up, hear me shout, ③ "Tip me o-ver and pour me out."

① Put right hand on hip to make a handle.
② Put left arm out with wrist bent down to make a spout.
③ Lean over to "pour" out of spout.

PROGRAM VII
Student pages 19-23

CONCEPTS: Signs for loud and soft
          Groups of three black keys
          Half note

MOTOR SKILLS: Responding to counting and clapping of quarter notes and half notes
          Responding to rhythm patterns

LISTENING: Hearing and repeating rhythm patterns
          Hearing loud and soft

ACTIVITIES

A.   Sing familiar songs, emphasizing loud and soft.

B.   Students complete page 19 as directed.

C.   Students complete work on pages 20 and 21.
Keyboard work: everyone chants "Three Little Monkeys" as students take turns playing the groups of three black keys, fingers or fist, up and down the keyboard, using right hand and left hand.
Students not playing should be clapping (KEEP IT SLOW!)
Play clusters, not separate keys.

D.   Use "Notes Can Go Up" poem, page 14, using groups of three black keys in clusters.

Students chant "High-Middle-Low" poem, page 5, while playing clusters on the groups of three black keys with fists. Three students could play this, being high, middle, low. (See "High-Middle-Low" song, page 33.)

E.   After completing page 22 students may play "leap frog" saying "bears, monkeys" as they play.

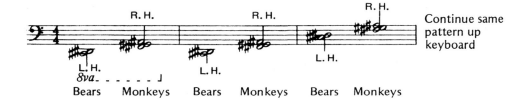

(Additional Black Key Songs - 47)

F.   Have the students use clusters of the three black keys to make rhythm patterns to suggest different sounds (car horns, rain drops, music box, horses, soldiers).

G.   Sing "Old McDonald", page 43, using high-low loud-soft animal sounds. After singing it together, each student could make one animal sound.

H.   On page 23 compare half note to quarter note. Emphasize the white appearance of note.
To clap half note, clap on ONE and squeeze hands together on TWO.
Students can make rhythm patterns of half notes and quarter notes on chalkboard, flannel board or plastic note boards. Clap the patterns.
Teach "Half Note March", page 43.

DAILY HOME ASSIGNMENTS for student and parent

1.   Notice loud and soft sounds around you.

2.   Student should practice playing the groups of three black keys up and down the keyboard, chanting "Three Little Monkeys", sometimes all right hand, sometimes all left hand. Also play in leap-frog fashion, LH, RH, LH, RH.

3.   Student should play each group of black keys up and down the keyboard, chanting "Bears Monkeys", using fists.

4.   Help student draw quarter notes and half notes. Both of you clap them. To clap a half note, clap on ONE and squeeze hands together on TWO.

Old MacDonald

Old Mac-Don-ald had a farm, E I E I O! And on that farm he

had some chicks, E I E I O! With a chick chick here and a

chick chick there, Here a chick there a chick, Ev-'ry-where a chick chick,

Old Mac - Don - ald had a farm, E I E I O!

Half Note March

B. GLASSCOCK

Half note marching 1-2 1-2 Half note marching 1-2 1-2

Half note marching 1-2 1-2 All a - round.

PROGRAM VIII
Student page 24

CONCEPTS: Recognition of rhythm patterns
Counting
MOTOR SKILLS: Responding to rhythm patterns by moving the body to the rhythm of songs
LISTENING: Hearing rhythms and melodies that tell what the songs are about

ACTIVITIES

A. Teacher draws rhythm patterns on the chalkboard. Have each student select a pattern for the other students to clap and count. ALWAYS count the rhythm pattern aloud.
Have the students take turns being the teacher and pointing to the notes of the pattern as the others clap and count. Check for left to right reading.
Have students draw rhythm patterns on chalkboard or newsprint. Clap or count.

B. Teach "Here We Go Round the Mulberry Bush", page 45. Have students decide how to act out each verse of the song to fit the rhythm of the music. Have students make up other verses, such as "This is the way we roller skate...early in the morning."

C. Teach "Did You Ever See A Lassie", page 45. Have students clap the pulse (first beat of each measure), using wide swings of their arms to the right and left.
At the phrase "go this way and that way" have one student make motions (stepping, tapping knees, shaking head), having everyone copy the motion when the phrase is repeated.
Be sure that every student has the chance to be the leader. With a little practice the students will be able to match their motions to the pulse of the song.

DAILY HOME ASSIGNMENTS for student and parent

1. Play black key clusters up the keyboard in quarter note rhythm saying "one one one one", fingers or fists. GO SLOWLY.

2. Student should draw some quarter note and half note rhythm patterns to clap and count.

3. Sing "Old McDonald" adding sounds other than animals - baby, clock, typewriter - anything that makes a sound. These can get a little silly - that's okay.

4. Review keyboard activities from past weeks: Bobby-Bonnie, Monkeys, High-Middle-Low, stories.

Mulberry Bush

1. Here we go 'round the mul-ber-ry bush, The mul-ber-ry bush, The mul-ber-ry bush.

Here we go 'round the mul-ber-ry bush, so ear-ly in — the morn-ing.

Verse: 1. This is the way we wash our clothes...on a Monday morning
2. This is the way we iron our clothes...Tuesday
3. This is the way we scrub the floor...Wednesday

Did You Ever See a Lassie?

Did you ev - er see a las - sie, a las - sie, a

las - sie, Did you ev - er see a las - sie go this way and

that? Go this way and that way, go this way and

that way. Did you ev - er see a las - sie go this way and that?

(PVII-C)

PROGRAM IX
Student Pages 25-26

CONCEPTS: Line and space notes

MOTOR SKILLS: Reinforcement of responding with a steady beat

LISTENING: Listening for familiar melodies

ACTIVITIES

A. Have students stand "on" the lines and "in" the spaces on the floor staff.
Using numbers written on construction paper squares, have students put numbers on the proper lines and in the proper spaces.
Have students put notes on lines and spaces of floor staff.
Have students draw space notes and line notes on chalkboard and on paper.

Help students complete page 25 as directed.
Have students pretend their heads are the note heads; for space notes have them put one hand under chin and the other on top of head. For line notes, have them put their hands across the face with fingers overlapping to make a line.

B. To review rhythm patterns:
1. Clap "echo pattern." Teacher claps a pattern, students repeat it.
2. Have a game. Students earn one point for each echo pattern clapped correctly.
3. Change the response. Clap the rhythm pattern then have students respond by doing the pattern on a rhythm instrument, two black keys, three black keys.

C. In preparation for page 26, have some quarter notes cut and ready to use. (Saves lesson time. Students could cut their own at home.)
Direct the note placement.

D. See LISTENING SUGGESTIONS page 48.

DAILY HOME ASSIGNMENTS for student and parent

Continue to spend music time together. Encourage your child to listen for different sounds and to respond to different rhythms. Experiment with keyboard sounds - up-down, high-low, loud-soft, black-white.

Give many compliments.

BLACK KEY SONGS

For each of the Black Key Songs the notes with stems that go up (♩) are to be played with the right hand. The notes with stems that go down (♩) are to be played with the left hand. Two or three notes with one stem (♫) are to be played at the same time.

For songs that go up, always start at the lowest group (the one furthest to your left) on the keyboard. For songs that go down, always start at the highest group (the one furthest to your right) on your keyboard.

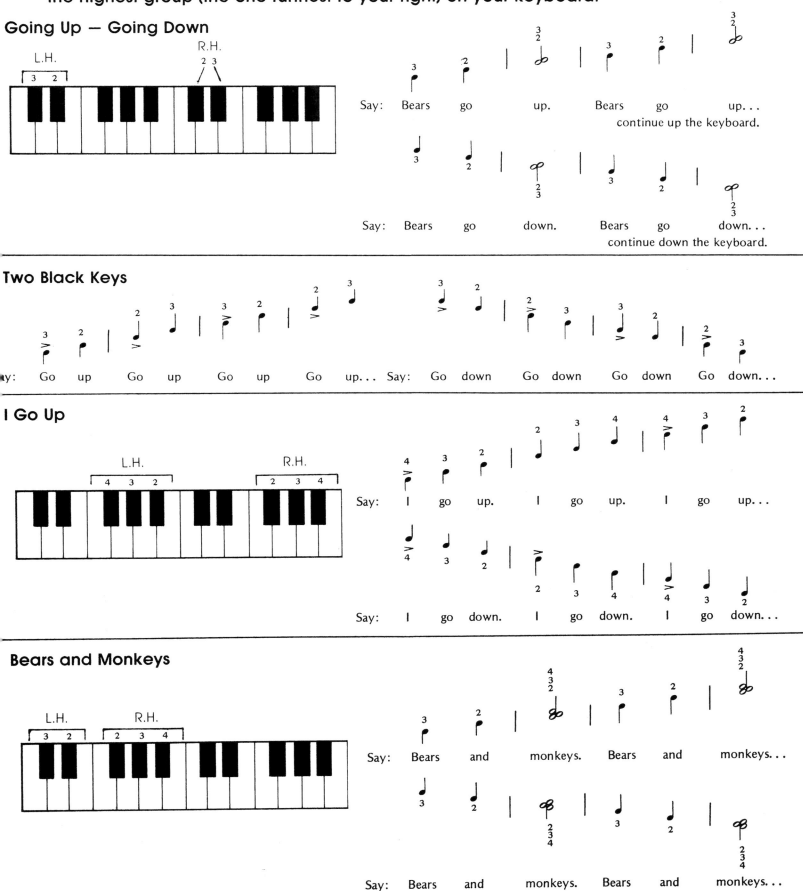

Going Up — Going Down

Two Black Keys

I Go Up

Bears and Monkeys

LISTENING SUGGESTIONS

Program Three:
      MEMORIES OF CHILDHOOD
      by Octavia Pinto

Program Four:
      PETER AND THE WOLF
      by Prokofiev
      SORCERER'S APPRENTICE
      by Dukas
      CINDERELLA SUITE
      by Prokofiev

Program Five:
      Dances from THE NUTCRACKER SUITE
      by Tchaikovsky
        If the students are not familiar
      with the story, tell them a bit
      about it. Explain who is dancing
      each dance.
      Let them dance to the music.

Program Nine:
      CHILDREN'S SYMPHONY
      by Hal McDonald
      Listen for familiar melodies.
      First movement:
          LONDON BRIDGE
          BAA, BAA, BLACK SHEEP
      Second movement:
          O, DEAR, WHAT CAN THE MATTER BE?
      Third movement:
          JINGLE BELLS
          FARMER IN THE DELL
      Fourth movement:
          THE HONEY BEE
          SNOW IS FALLING IN MY GARDEN

ADDITIONAL SUGGESTED SINGING AND LISTENING MATERIALS

1. THE SMALL MUSICIAN SERIES

2. BOWMAR ORCHESTRAL LIBRARY
   from Bowmar Music and Records
   Belwin-Mills Publishing Corp., Miami, FL 33014

3. GAMES AND ACTIVITIES FOR EARLY CHILDHOOD
   by Margaret Athey and Gwen Hotchkiss
   from Parker Publishing Co., West Nyack, N.Y.